Secrets

about

Money

That Put *You* At Risk

The Basic Things About

Money and Wealth

You Must Know

And Probably Do Not

---

by

Michael J. McKay

Host of

RadioFreeMarket.com

This is the first printing of

Secrets About Money That Put You at Risk

Published by

**Radio Free Market
February 2010**

Printed in the United States of America

Radio Free Market
202 South Second St
Fairfield, Iowa 52556
www.SecretsAboutMoney.net

ISBN: 978-0-9826615-0-5

"This book is your place to start on your journey to Monetary Intelligence."

Dr. Mark Thornton
Former Asst Superintendent of Banking
State of Alabama

Dedication

To my sweet daughters, Kelly and Marina, so that
they may create their Wealthiest Future.

With Love,
Dad

Contents

Foreword

During the final days of the Soviet Empire I was an eyewitness to the importance of understanding '*How Money Works*' and the terrible cost that comes when people do not have a basic grasp of this vital foundational knowledge.

The demise of Soviet Socialism was caused to a large extent by the collapse of its financial system: runaway inflation coupled with mass shortages of almost everything.

It was to no one's surprise when anti-socialist reformers sought to reign in government power they looked to solve the money problem first.

"Moscow held unlimited power to flood their economies with cheap money, and to fund itself as an imperial power lording it over other peoples. That had to end before the market economy could be restored"

> - wrote Llewellyn Rockwell at that time.

The importance of our understanding the nature, functions and consequences of fiat money and fractional reserve banking is imperative for any intelligent citizen.

One of the best gateways to such an understanding is an outstanding introduction to monetary economics "*Secrets About Money That Put You At Risk*" written by Michael McKay.

It provides concise but deep analysis and explanation of the nature of value, money, inflation, and wealth and their intrinsic interdependence.

It is a must read for everyone interested in economics and concerned with our government's irresponsible monetary policy. I recommend it with great enthusiasm!

Dr. Yuri Maltsev
Professor of Economics
Carthage College
February 2010

Chapter 1

<u>Why did this happen?</u>

In 2007 and 2008 Homeowners in California, Nevada, Florida and many other states saw the value of their homes plummet – much to their surprise.

What did a lot of really smart people not know or not understand? [1]

<u>Why does this happen?</u>

Business failures are a normal part of the economic landscape.

In fact failures are *supposed* to happen!

Every entrepreneur must forecast – that means guess – about the future of their market in order to be, they hope, profitable. When they are wrong they go out of business.

Just like everything else in life, *some are better at forecasting than others.* Some will guess more correctly than others. It happens all the time.

So why does it happen **en masse** every so often?

---

[1] For an excellent understanding please read *Meltdown: A Free-Market Look at Why the Stock Market Collapsed, the Economy Tanked, and Government Bailouts Will Make Things Worse,* by Dr. Thomas E. Woods, Jr., (Regnery, 2009). Download the **Radio Free Market** Interview with Dr. Woods at http://www.radiofreemarket.com/?q=node/13 .

Why do so many entrepreneurs forecast incorrectly <u>at the same time</u>, which results in the Widespread Closing of Businesses, Massive Unemployment and Debilitating Economic Depressions? [2]

The details of each of these examples are different but the central reason is the same.

There are distinct and important differences between:

- **Deep *Systemic* Understanding** about money and how it works, and

- **Merely *Functional* Knowledge**.

An unfair example would be that *Merely Functional Knowledge* allows you to drive a car, where as a *Deep Systemic Understanding* would be to understand how a car's engine operates and - importantly - *to recognize early any signs of it malfunctioning.*

I say that is an 'unfair example' because – with a car – most of us understand that when the dashboard 'Oil Light' is flashing we better attend to the engine.

With Money most of us do not even know which 'dials and dashboard indicators' we should be looking at.

To make this point another way let me ask this question:

---

[2] For an excellent understanding please read:
Economic Depressions: Their Cause and Cure, by Murray Rothbard
(http://mises.org/store/product.aspx?ProductId=591)

Q: What do all of these have in common?

- The ABC's and stories of Dick and Jane.
- Basic Math
- The Guitar Chords C,D,G and F
- Two Basic Dance Steps

Answer: All will get you **by** – until they don't, until you get into a more complicated situation.

All are sufficient for basic function.

All *lack* a deeper competence and limit your ability to deal with more complex life.

All will ultimately cause you to make a mistake when you get to the end of your 'functional knowledge'.

All are like playing the 'piano of life' with one or two fingers. It greatly limits the 'songs' you can play – particularly if life suddenly requires you to play with more than one or two fingers!

So what are the basic indicators that we should know about and be watching when it comes to money?

I *would like* to tell you that in the next few pages you will learn all the Deeper Systemic Knowledge that you need to know. But I cannot.

I can tell you that in the next few pages – no matter where you are on the learning scale - you will basically understand four of the most important things about money that most people do not know.

These four concepts are the key 'dials' that should be on your monetary dashboard, so to speak. You may never become an expert mechanic or economist but you <u>absolutely</u> need to know what these 'dials' are <u>and how to read them</u>.

Also, it is important to know that having this Greater Systemic Knowledge does not completely insulate you from those who have Central Control over our Money and Banking System and the damage they can wreak.

<u>But</u> '*Forewarned is Forearmed*' - having this knowledge at least gives you a fighting chance of taking protective measures *that can reduce your risk*. You also – if you choose to study further, invest wisely and are lucky – could even make a profit.

At a minimum, having this Greater Systemic Knowledge will allow you to better and more knowledgably navigate the Money World you are in.

Without this Knowledge you are like a ship without a rudder.

With this Knowledge you at least can steer.

And based on the Storms that are a'brewing and the Rocks in the path of our current Money System – this basic knowledge is indispensable.

Later, I will refer you to additional resources that will deepen your Systemic understanding if you want to take your knowledge further.

Chapter 2

<u>The Big Four</u>

It is time for you to understand four of the most overlooked – **most basic –** and most important interlocking aspects of money. Understanding these four concepts – and how they interrelate - is essential to understanding *how money works*:

- **Legal Tender Law versus Competing Currencies,**

- **Fiat Money,**

- **Inflation, and**

- **Fractional Reserve Banking.**

I consider these basic money concepts **mandatory systemic understanding** for all who ever handle money – and that actually means everyone, not just professionals.

What follows will give you a basic grasp of these key concepts. Afterward, there is a list of additional resources that will expand your understanding to whatever depth you desire. The next few pages are very important for you. I hope they will permanently improve your understanding about Money.

Chapter 3

What is Better?
Legal Tender or
Competing Currencies?

Legal Tender Laws mean you must use this thing the government declares to be money – **and only this thing as money** - or you are breaking the law.

But, you ask, what are you talking about? I only know this one thing, these green bills and pot-metal coins, as money.

Unless you are an older person chances are you do not remember different money than we have now. But when I was a paper boy in 1964 and 1965 I was already aware that some of the dimes were 90% pure Silver and the others were pot-metal. I was aware that some of the quarters were 90%, then 40% Silver and that *it made a difference.*

In fact, throughout history there have mostly been competing currencies where folks would pay different prices depending on what money they were using – because each money was worth something different. [3]

Competing currencies ultimately serve the public. Because it is true that everybody needs money, people – if left to choose for themselves – **will pick**

---

[3] Ref: http://www.fairfieldweekly.com/article.cfm?aid=11757 Accessed Aug 16, 2009

the best money and eventually that will become the most common money.

In a Free Market we would have competing currencies and **folks would discover what kind of money works the best** – Money that retained its value over time and was useable with the largest number of buyers and sellers.

The Best Money – the one most folks would eventually use if it were not otherwise imposed on them by a government - would be a money that worked well if you wanted to save it, because it did not lose its purchasing power, and would work well if you wanted to use it to buy something in a far off land – because it would have a near universal value as a 'medium of exchange'; as something that just about anyone, anywhere would accept as money.

This is how Gold and Silver have traditionally become the **dominant money** – they are what the *Market Itself* selects if not forced to use something else by a government.

Legal Tender Laws make us use something for money even if something else may be better.
Legal Tender Laws require us to use this one thing – particularly for the payment of taxes - for money and do not allow other competing forms of money **or we can be punished.**

So what is the penalty?

During the French Revolution it was the guillotine.[4] During the American Revolution you could be imprisoned, or have your property confiscated, for not accepting the soon-to-be-worthless 'Continental'. [5]

Fortunately for us today it is not quite so severe. In the USA the penalties today are the Potential Cancellation of Debts and even Imprisonment.

Here is an example of our USA legal tender law penalty:

I shovel the snow from your sidewalk or mow your lawn at the agreed price of $10.

I, being the seller of my service, show up at your door with the job well done and my hand out.

You, being the buyer of my service, try to give me a $10 Federal Reserve Note, which is currently our Legal *Tender* Money.

Please notice this word "**Tender**"; it means to "offer".

So when you offer the $10 Federal Reserve Note you are making a "Legal *Tender*" which is the same as saying "Legal *Offer*" to pay me.

---

[4] *Fiat Money Inflation in France.* A.D.White. Available free online at http://mises.org/books/inflationinfrance.pdf pp 42-43 Accessed August 16, 2009

[5] *A Short History of Paper Money and Banking.* Wm M. Gouge. Available free online at http://mises.org/books/shorthistorypapermoney.pdf pp 29. Accessed August 16, 2009. **Note in particular the paragraph:** "Congress began, as early as Jan 11th, 1776, to hold-up and recommend this *maxim of mania-ism*, when continental money was but five months old. Congress then resolved that 'whoever should refuse to receive in payment continental bills, should be declared and treated as an enemy of his country, and be precluded from intercourse with its inhabitants,' i.e. should be *outlawed*: which is the severest penalty (except life and limb,) known to our laws." {italics in the original}

But, I frown and say:

"Actually I do not accept $10 Federal Reserve Notes. I only accept _____ (*here you can insert anything else: pesos, pop tarts, gold – anything other than Federal Reserve Notes*).

And I will only accept these (pesos, pop tarts or gold)."

<u>Here comes the problem.</u>

If I say,

"I am sorry but I will only accept (pesos, pop tarts, gold)"

.....*you do not have to pay me.*

In fact, if I am really stubborn about this and try to <u>make you</u> (as in 'sue you') to pay me in pesos, pop tarts or gold **the Courts won't make you pay me.**

They will instead tell *me* I must accept the Legal Tender Money (currently Federal Reserve Notes) *or I will get nothing*.

Furthermore, if I never change my mind to finally accept the Federal Reserve Notes **the debt is eventually canceled (through the Statute of Limitations)**.[6]

This is how a Stubborn *Seller* can get penalized.

---

[6] *Principles of Economics*, Ralph H. Blodgett, New York, Rinehart & Co. Third Printing 1947, p 438

A Stubborn *Buyer* cannot make a Restaurant accept his Pesos for the pizza he just ate. If he refuses to pay his tab in Federal Reserve Notes then *he could even go to jail.*

In other words, buyers and sellers are *required* to use Federal Reserve Notes "**for all debts, public and private**" as it is printed on the bills in your pocket or purse.

Go ahead and take one out - look at it now to see.

Chapter 4

<u>Fiat Money</u>

The word 'Fiat' means '**An Authoritative but Arbitrary *Decree*'.**[7]

In the USA today our current currency (we have had several in our history) is Fiat Money.

This is "money because we, the government, say it is."

Legal Tender Laws enforce that declaration.

In other words, if you do not want to use this Fiat Money as money, too bad, we, the government, are going to make you anyway.

All is well.....as long as it works or until '**others'** change their mind.

In order for Fiat Money to continue to be valued as a '**Form of Exchange'** and '**Store of Value'**, which are essential requirements for money to be money, three conditions must exist:

1) **A government power must remain that government power *indefinitely.***
My nephew, while serving in Iraq, came upon a warehouse of Iraqi Currency with Saddam's face all

---

[7] Merriam-Webster Dictionary of Law 1996
http://dictionary.reference.com/cite.html?qh=fiat&ia=mwlaw

over it. He contacted me to find out what it was worth. I called several professional currency traders who confirmed my opinion that since Saddam's Government was no more, neither was his fiat money.

It was only worth the paper itself.

2) **No one that has government authority changes their mind that this particular piece of decreed fiat money should have its value changed – *as in lowered.***

Note that this happens every time the Federal Reserve prints new dollars because each newly printed dollar lowers the value of each one already in your pocket.

3) **(And this is Vital)** *Other* **Nations must continue to believe in a Fiat Money's Value.**

When a significant number of other Nations will not accept a Country's money in exchange (think Zimbabwe) **then the Fiat Party is over** for that particular Country's money.

Please note the picture on the next page; this sign hangs above a restroom facility at a border station between South Africa and Zimbabwe.[8] It shows that when a Fiat Money becomes worthless it is not even usable for this basic human function.

---

[8] http://freakonomics.blogs.nytimes.com/2008/12/18/freak-shots-when-money-goes-down-the-toilet/ (accessed February 12, 2010)

Since:

a) There has never been a country or empire in the history of the world that has existed intact since the beginning of civilization, and

b) We have seen a consistent tendency of government leaders to change their minds and directions over the ages, as well as outright debase a currency via various forms of *dilution and declaration*, and

c) We are currently seeing our US Dollar shrinking in perceived value at an alarming rate around the world, it is easy to understand that Fiat Money is highly undependable.

In fact, the Historical Record shows that **every example of Fiat Money has eventually ended with it being reduced to the status of 'worthless';** for example, our first currency which became "Not worth a Continental", the French 'Assignat', or the 1923 meltdown of the German 'Reichsmark', to mention just three.

It is worthwhile for every citizen, young and old, to learn the details why history does not paint a pretty picture of Fiat Money's prospects for their future.

Below is a chart of the US Dollar's declining purchasing power since 1913, the year the Federal Reserve was formed and when we started the road toward having a pure Fiat Money in the USA.

Does this look like the direction you want your money to go? [9]

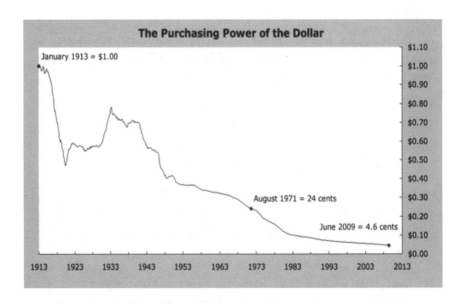

The Purchasing Power of the Dollar

January 1913 = $1.00

August 1971 = 24 cents

June 2009 = 4.6 cents

[9] *Source: Bureau of Labor Statistics.* Used with permission of the American Institute for Economic Research http://www.aier.org/research/commentaries/1826-the-long-goodbye-the-declining-purchasing-power-of-the-dollar Accessed August 15, 2009

Chapter 5

Inflation 101

Most of us think we know only too well what Inflation is.

Just ask any Senior Citizen on a fixed income watching – **with alarm** - their grocery and energy bill rise higher and higher year after year.

Or just ask anyone trying to make ends meet on a tight budget. Food, gasoline, insurance, basic needs, virtually everything is constantly more expensive.

Prices always seem to be going up.

Why is this happening?

It is important to know that Price Inflation (what we see) is caused by Money Inflation which is what the public really needs to learn about.

Monetary Inflation **occurs every time the Federal Reserve prints a new dollar bill**. It also occurs **every time a bank lends more money than it has on hand.** [10]

These two things cause each previously printed/created dollar to be worth *less*; it *dilutes* each dollar's value.

---

[10] This is actually legal and is called **'Fractional Reserve Banking'** where banks create money literally out of thin air. We will address this in the next chapter.

Think of pouring water into milk and you get the picture.

Every time the Fed "lowers interest rates" it is also printing/creating new dollar bills thereby inflating the monetary supply.

When this happens you should immediately think:

"My paycheck will now buy <u>less</u>. My savings are now worth <u>less</u>."

The Federal Reserve has been doing this very thing since 1913.

In the last 95 years our **Purchasing Power** - <u>which is the key thing we all want</u> – has dropped over 95%. To put it another way, something that cost 5 cents in 1913 now costs $1.00 or more. You may have wondered where Penny Candy went; now you know.

It is also important that we all understand the <u>sequence</u> of Inflation.

First, dollars are printed, or loaned into existence, which dilute the Purchasing Power of each previous dollar created.

Then everybody, from producers to processors and finally consumers see prices go up.

Consumers are the last to see it.

Consumers have a natural impulse to blame the stores or businesses from which they buy, because that store or business is where they <u>see</u> the prices 'going up'.

But this is wrong.

Stores and businesses **must**, in order to continue being stores and businesses, cover the higher costs they experience.

<u>First</u>, stores and businesses experience higher prices, <u>then</u> they pass them on.

Consumers are left holding the bag.

In summary:

Inflation means an increase of the <u>Money Supply</u> which <u>then</u> causes each unit of money to become worth less and therefore to be able to buy less.

Prices rise _after_ Money is inflated.

Chapter 6

<u>Fractional Reserve Banking and Horse Racing</u>

<u>Important Fact:</u>

Fractional Reserve Banking is the primary way <u>Inflation</u> is created in our economy.

Some feel this topic should not be brought to the public's attention; and some feel the public should not be concerned because the system has various checks and balances that, so far, have allowed it, until recently, to continue relatively unscathed. Some may even say I am trying to disparage the fine and honest people in our local banks which I *emphatically* am not trying to do.

I feel the public should *always* be concerned about our money *and* how it works. This essential topic has been out of the public discussion for far too long.

Here's how Fractional Reserve Banking works:

1) Every bank, large and small, takes in deposits **and then lends out many multiples of these deposits.**

Note that this new loaned money is *created out of thin air.*

Note that banks lend out many times more than they can deliver to their depositors if everyone wanted their money out at the same time.

21

This is like selling the same horse to three different people because they want to ride it on different days of the week. This idea works until the three "owners" meet and decide to have a horse race!

Obviously, this in its very essence is fraud. Two or more people cannot own the same thing at the same time; this is a bedrock principle of property rights.

2) This creation of new money by the banks **has the same effect as the Federal Reserve printing new dollar bills, <u>which is to reduce the value of all other dollars already in circulation</u>**.

This, then, reduces our precious Purchasing Power which hurts everyone, particularly the elderly and poor.

3) **This 'creating money out of thin air' is the true origin of Inflation.**

This *inflating of the supply of money* – "monetary inflation" – *later* becomes known to us as "price inflation" as the newly created money works its way through the economy.

4) Fractional Reserve Banking and the printing of new money by the Federal Reserve has been the basis **of a policy of *Planned Inflation*** that has reduced our Purchasing Power 95% in the past 95 years.

The current bailout of major banks by the Federal Reserve's <u>massive</u> emergency creation of new money is going to have a very strong inflationary impact on us all.

Note that in the period ahead you are going to see price inflation dramatically surge ahead. <u>Everything</u> is going to cost you more.

This arrangement has been totally legal, and has been made to work for many decades via various manipulations.

However, that does not make the practice of Fractional Reserve Banking right, or ethical, or guaranteed to work in the future.

In fact, it does not need to be this way. [11]

---

[11] Rothbard, Murray. *What has Government Done To Our Money?* (Auburn, AL, Mises Institute, 2008) Available free online at http://mises.org/books/whathasgovernmentdone.pdf

Chapter 7

An Important Question to ask Your Public School Board and How to Get Ready to Talk to Them

Why is it that Money is:

a) *The thing* **that most of us worry about the most, and**

b) *Is the thing* **that you understand and were educated in school about the LEAST?**

Hmmmmmm?????????????

Why is it that we do not teach to our kids the comparative schools of economic thought: Austrian, Keynesian, Monetarist, and Marxist - in depth or even at all?

Why do otherwise educated people say (tragically):

"I really do not understand Economics."

?????

I would submit to you that **we have better offerings in 'Drivers Education'** than in understanding the much more important topic of *What is Money and How it Works.*

Now is the time for all of us to learn **what we should have in Grade School and High School.**

Do not fear this; it is NOT rocket science.

You can readily understand the key concepts by doing four things:

1) Please go to the **Education** page of www.radiofreemarket.com and start with the *Beginner* section under *Getting a Grip*.

2) Please read the book "*Whatever Happened to Penny Candy*" by Richard Maybury which you can purchase at http://www.bluestockingpress.com/whatever-happened-penny-candy.htm .

This will teach you other foundational concepts of Money, Inflation and how it relates to Law and Ethics.

3) Please work your way up to Phase II on our **Education** page at www.radiofreemarket.com .

There is a wealth of information which is designed to give you **Basic Systemic Knowledge**.

4) Please go to mises.org and start your own self-education process, most of which is free of charge. This site will take you as deep as you care to go.

Let us remember – and learn from - the 1829 quote from President John Quincy Adams which is still relevant today:

" ... All the perplexities, confusion and distress in America arise,

- **not from the defects in their constitution or confederation,**

- **not from want of honor or virtue,**

- **so much as from <u>down right ignorance</u> of the nature of coin, credit and circulation..."**

Yes, ignorance about money may be widespread, but it is curable – one person at a time. And you now know more about money than most people in society today.

You are not fully "cured" yet, but you at least can read the dials on your economic dashboard which should be a great advantage to you in the times to come.

Now you are ready for the next step. Now that you understand the *Big Four*: **Fiat Money, Legal Tender Laws, Fractional Reserve Banking and, most important of all, Inflation.**

It is now time to take the next step, to unravel the most common confusion that people have about **Wealth, Value and Money.**

Chapter 8

<u>Wealth ≠ Value ≠ Money</u>

Recently, in the last few months of 2008 and early 2009, many people opened their mail to find that their Stock Portfolio's Value was cut in half, *or worse.*

General Motors, one of the Bluest of Blue Chips, **fell from $25 to under $2 in 12 months and fell from $52 over the last ten years.** [12]

As I write this (I started this section in March 2009) several of the Blue Chip Dow Stocks **are valued under $10** including Citicorp, General Electric, Alcoa, GM and Bank of America.

While this was happening to stock portfolios, homeowners from California to Florida **discovered that their Real Estate values had fallen, in some cases 30% to 50%, or more.** [13]

Truly these losses are massive and devastating.

Did these people experience a loss of *Wealth*?

---

[12] Price of GM Stock: $52.41 per share on January 27, 1999, $25.22 p/s Feb 20, 2008, $1.77 p/s on Feb 20, 2009. ref:
http://finance.yahoo.com/q/hp?s=GM&a=00&b=2&c=1999&d=02&e=3&f=2009&g=d&z=66&y=0 (accessed 3/04/09)
[13] See: http://www.latimes.com/business/la-fi-housing20-2009jan20,1,2250037.story (accessed 3/04/09)

The press would make it seem so. Headlines like the following were common:

Household wealth falls to record low

WASHINGTON - US household <u>wealth</u> fell in the third quarter by the most on record as property <u>values</u> and stock prices tumbled, highlighting the tattered state of consumer finances. Bloomberg News, December 12, 2008 [14] (underlining added)

To be sure many people are feeling poorer. **But did they lose _Wealth_ or did they just lose _Value_?**

<u>Question:</u> When do you know something is actually worth what you think it is?

<u>Answer:</u> **When you actually sell it.**

Prior to when we sell it we only _think_ we know what the Market will bear. **Selling it tells you, in fact, what it is worth.**

Whether it is a Pomeranian Puppy, a Boxcar of Ping Pong Balls or a pile of GM Stock, _Value_ **is not Wealth. Wealth we _have_.**

Value, or perhaps the better term is 'valuation', is what we _think_ we have.

But look closely.

The loss of VALUE is not the same thing as a loss in WEALTH, although they are connected.

---

[14]http://www.boston.com/business/articles/2008/12/12/household_wealth_falls_to_record_low/ (accessed 2/28/09)

All these people *assumed* they knew what their house was *worth*.

But as they all found out **its real worth is realized when it is actually sold.**

Until then it is only a guess.

To be sure, banks and governments take this *guess* and give out credit and charge taxes on what you, they and other professional 'assessors' guess what it is worth.

But in the final analysis, these guesses are only Valuations, and they can and do change, both Up and Down.

So let's summarize:

Value **is constantly subject to change.**

Chapter 9

<u>So, What is Wealth?</u>

By contrast to Value, which is constantly subject to change, **Wealth** – in it's broadest and most general sense – **is something that we actually have** *and will likely have tomorrow.*

In other words, Wealth sticks around.

Even though 'nothing lasts forever' you can depend on Wealth being there for a while. Your kitchen table is Wealth. Certainly your house, furniture, your car, your old guitar or wine collection is Wealth.

Value, by contrast, is something that <u>maybe</u> you can <u>convert</u> to Wealth.

You might be able to 'get' $50 per share for that stock but then again, if it was General Motors stock, maybe only $2.

At fifty bucks a share you could have converted 1000 shares of GM to a new Lexus, but at two bucks you might get a really old used pickup or a nifty new scooter.

Of course, the examples become more profound – and dire - when you add a zero.

If you had 10,000 shares of GM stock in 1999 you thought that your 'wealth' was over $500,000. If you were counting on that 'wealth' being there in 2009, when you were planning on retiring for example, you were left with under $20,000 with which to face your future.

Tragically, this is not a hypothetical example. It is happening over and over again right now.

Conversion of Value INTO Wealth is something we all assume we can do.

Or to put it another way, we assume the Value will be there and it is a *Store* of Wealth.

Well Value is just Value **and it changes all the time**. It is here today and maybe here tomorrow or maybe gone tomorrow.

Maybe Value will go up, in which case we get to convert it to even more and neater stuff. But maybe Value will go down as well.

So, we see that Wealth is something we actually *Realize,* <u>we actually have</u> *and can rely on having for a time.*

Value is only *Potentially* Realized, later – maybe.

Chapter 10

We Define Wealth in More Ways than One

In the examples above we talked about Wealth as if it only was connected to things like cars, stocks, and furniture. Indeed, these things can be – and indeed are - Wealth to us.

But there are actually two aspects to Wealth and both are important to us:

Objective-Tangible and Subjective-Intangible.

Both of these, what we will call **Total Wealth**, are important to us and we want both of these to be as lasting and permanent as possible.

First, let's discuss the **Objective-Tangible form of Wealth.**

This is all the Objective Valuable Stuff that we can put on an Accountant's Ledger Sheet.

These are all the things that we can own, use and sell if we want to. We know now that these things have a *Value* that we discover when we try to sell it to someone else. This is our **Tangible Wealth** and is what we usually are talking about when the whole topic of Wealth, Value and Money comes up. When your Accountant is adding up 'how wealthy' you are it is this category of Tangible Wealth that he is looking at; **he is looking at the numbers.**

But there are other Valuable Things in Life that your Accountant is <u>not</u> looking at, that are personal, private and actually aren't THINGS at all like Health, Love, Time With Your Family and many other Non-Money-Related things.

What about these *Intangible Wealth* elements?

Even though we can't put them on the Ledger Sheet they ADD to our Quality of Life and we <u>cherish</u> them; *they are Dear and Important to us* **and, maybe, are even more important than any - OR ALL - of our 'Stuff' put together.**

Indeed there are monks, recluses and sadhus that have few, if any, material possessions but that is exactly the way they want it. For them NOT owning things and being free of having to worry about material possessions is a condition that is most cherishable to them.

'*Wealth is Health*' is an old adage that anyone who has ever faced health challenges can attest.

The Tirukural, the Holy Book of the Tamil People of Southern India, has 1300 verses and many of them deal with the **different forms of Wealth** both tangible and intangible. Called the Kural, for short, it says that the personality quality of '*Industriousness*' is someone's '*real*' **form of Wealth** because those who possess industriousness can never really be poor.[15]

---

[15] Satguru Sivaya Subramuniyaswami, '*Weavers Wisdom, Ancient Precepts for a Perfect Life*' (India, Himalayan Academy, 1999) p. 145, Chp 60, v 600

Similarly it refers to **other intangible qualities** of *Compassion*[16] and *Mental Energy* [17] as being high forms of Wealth. Children, *'endowed with intelligence'*, is noted as a sweet form of Wealth desired by parents.[18]

Others have opined that *Carefree-ness* is the highest form of *Intangible* Wealth. Love and quality relationships – someone being there for me – for many is Wealth above all others.

Many of the things we would call Intangible Wealth we can give away <u>and not lose at the same time.</u> When you share with me your Wealth of Knowledge <u>you still have</u> your Wealth of Knowledge. When you sell me your table and chairs <u>you no longer have them</u> – you give them or sell them AWAY, they go bye-bye, and then you don't have them anymore.

It is important to not get confused by this basic fact of life; we all really want BOTH, a combination of things that are <u>external</u> to us – Stuff and Things to some degree or another – mixed with what is also very <u>internal</u>, private and important to us.

The sum of both the internal and the external is what we could call **Total Wealth**; *it includes both the Intangible and the Tangible.*

Total Wealth is being able to go to bed at night, being comfortable, feeling safe, knowing that in the morning you will have clothes to wear and items in

---

[16] Ibid, p. 141, Chp 58 v 572 and Chp 76 v 757
[17] Ibid, p. 145, Chp 60 v 592
[18] Ibid, p. 23, Chp 7 v 61

the refrigerator with which to have breakfast; wealth is the cups and plates and spoons we own as well.

We can project into the future with some reliability that the bed is going to be there, the clothes are going to be there and the food is going to be there.

That is called 'Security' and for some – even maybe most of us – is a very important form of Intangible Wealth.

In a very real sense **Total Wealth** is like having our own **River of Comforts** that we have and can project that we will have into the future; as it flows we just pay attention to our River and nurse it to become bigger and deeper.

We all seem to be on the path to expand what we have, what we want.

Chapter 11

The Value of Money – *itself* – Can Change

It is a curious condition of Human Nature that we all, always and in all things, **project out into the longer term future the experiences from our recent past** that include up to and including now.

This is that very dangerous aspect of the Human Psyche that sets us up for **Panics** and **Manias** and **bad investment decisions**.

It is vital to understand how ephemeral Values are. They can go up, which they typically do slowly, or they can go down as they often do quickly.

To borrow a verse from the Kural, Values come to one slowly *'like the gathering of a theater crowd. Its dispersal is sudden, like that same crowd departing'*. [19]

So it is very important to remember that Value and Wealth are not the same. This of course applies to Money as well. **Money itself can lose its Value.**

If you recently held all your money in Icelandic Krona you were wiped out. The Value of the Icelandic Money

---

[19] Ibid, p. 83, Chp 34 v 332

went effectively to zero in October 2008 when foreign banks "no longer accepted it".[20]

Or, of course, you could have held the world's worst currency, currently the Zimbabwe Dollar, where each Note comes ***with an expiration date printed on it!*** (Please notice the amounts are $10Million and $250Million Dollar Notes!)

---

[20]See:http://www.nytimes.com/2008/10/10/business/worldbusiness/10icebank.html?fta=y (accessed 3/04/09)

Remember this: **if prices go up the purchasing power has *already* gone down** and that Money has lost some of its value.

Also, it is possible that the Value of Money can GO UP as well which is called 'Price Deflation' where prices go down and your money's value increases. This is a boon to Savers and the Elderly on fixed incomes.

You hear a lot in the Press that Price Deflation is BAD and how the Government is trying hard to avoid it but – think about it:

Who Benefits When Prices Go Down?

You do, the consumer.

Every Consumer benefits if their Money buys more, if their Purchasing Power becomes *stronger*.

We see this **when Prices go Down; then the money in your pocket can buy more.**

Look around and you will see that some things actually have become cheaper **and better** over time: Computers, TV's, heck most Electronics, as well as Lasik Eye Surgery and many Plastic Surgery Procedures all cost less while the quality, features and benefits have all increased dramatically.

So what is the problem with that?

Because our Central Bankers (and the not-yet-educated in the Press and Media) tell us that 'Deflation is Bad' you need to learn the basics of why Deflation is not to be feared and why **Inflation is really the _bad_ thing**. [21]

The best way to learn the basics on Deflation is to read a short book by Dr. Jorg Guido Hulsmann titled *'Deflation and Liberty'*. You can even read it for free. [22]

It is vitally important to recognize that a Money's Value can, and usually does, change over time.

Money, different kinds of Money, have different Values and how we know this is by observing the **Purchasing Power of that Money**.

---

[21] See Chapter 5 above, *Inflation 101*

[22] Hulsmann, Jorg Guido *'Deflation and Liberty'* (Auburn, AL, Mises Institute, 2008) Read this book at http://mises.org/books/deflationandliberty.pdf

Chapter 12

<u>Money, Value and Wealth are Interconnected but</u>

<u>Are *Not* the Same Thing</u>

<u>– and we need to think about them differently.</u>

It deeply concerns me how often these interlocking concepts of Wealth, Value and Money are confused by people.

People often think that having a great deal of money is *having wealth.*

Well having a lot of money *maybe* is 'having wealth', but only if the *Value* of the Money is maintained, if indeed the Money is a real **Store of Wealth**, if it is Sound and Lasting Money.

Sound and Lasting means money where the **Purchasing Power** - at a minimum - is maintained over time.

But if the Purchasing Power of the Money is falling due to price inflation or general devaluation of the Money, **then....where is the Wealth?**

Without a doubt, Sound Money is a *key* aspect of long term Wealth for all of us.

The Biggest Goal we all have is **Having and Maintaining Wealth**. Wealth is something we want to *have and hold*, and *continue* to have and hold.

In order to have *Wealth that Sticks* we need:

1. Sound Money in order for **our money to be a Store of Wealth** where our Purchasing Power is protected and not eroded.

2. We need to be aware that **Value is something that *changes constantly*** because each new potential buyer subjectively decides if it is worth what we think it is.

The Value of Things (which includes our Money and our Stuff) can go up as well as down.

We cannot be complacent to think we 'know' the Value of a thing at any given moment. Assuming that old guitar or that pile of stock is worth 'a bundle' is something that **you can only know for sure when you sell it.**

Prior to that time you are guessing.

3. Total Wealth is the sum of two forms: **Objective-Tangible and Subjective-Intangible Wealth.**

The Objective Stuff is what we can use and, if we want to, sell – we can attach numbers that have a Price-Value to these things.

The most important thing to remember about Objective Wealth is that it's Price-Value – it's worth - is determined by the NEXT buyer and what he or she thinks it is worth.

The Subjective Aspect of Wealth includes all those Personal *Qualities* and *Conditions* that we feel are important in our life. It is hard to put a price on these things because they are what make life worth living in the first place.

It is very important that we be clear about ***our individual definition of Total Wealth*** which <u>is always our own personal recipe</u>.

My definition is not yours; I will want a different combination of Objective and Subjective things than you will. My mixture of desired Tangibles and Intangibles will differ from yours.

How big I want my River of Comforts is maybe bigger or smaller than yours. You may want **more** free time and think that having time to garden is your highest form of Wealth. I may want to own the big swimming pool because laying in it – **more** of the time - makes me *feel* wealthy.

It is simply our Nature, our Natural Tendency, to want *'**More**'* out of life.

We can't help it; it's how we are wired.

I hope you now have a better understanding how the interlocking pieces of **Wealth, Value and Money** fit together.

Understanding how **these pieces are different, yet fit together,** will better prepare you to pursue your own recipe of *'More in Life'* and try to make your life as complete as you can.

Important Resources that will Deepen Your Understanding of How Money Works.

Essentials of Economics, by Faustino Ballve
Read *Free* Here: http://mises.org/books/ballve.pdf

Deflation and Liberty, by Jorg Guido Hulsmann
Read *Free* Here: http://mises.org/books/deflationandliberty.pdf

The Case Against the Fed, by Murray Rothbard
Read *Free* Here: http://mises.org/books/fed.pdf

Economic Depressions: Their Cause and Cure,
by Murray Rothbard   **Read *Free* Here:**
http://mises.org/books/economic_depressions_rothbard.pdf

What has Government Done To Our Money?,
by Murray Rothbard
Read *Free* Here: http://mises.org/books/whathasgovernmentdone.pdf

Fiat Money Inflation in France, by A.D.White.
Read *Free* Here: http://mises.org/books/inflationinfrance.pdf

A Short History of Paper Money and Banking,
by Wm M. Gouge.
Read *Free* Here: http://mises.org/books/shorthistorypapermoney.pdf

The Concise Guide to Economics, by Jim Cox
Available at:
http://mises.org/store/Concise-Guide-to-Economics-The-P193.aspx

Not a Zero Sum Game, by Manuel Ayau
Read *Free* Here: http://mises.org/books/game.pdf

Early Speculative Bubbles & Increases in the Supply of Money, by Douglas French
Read *Free* Here: http://mises.org/Books/bubbles.pdf

* Note: all of these excellent resources – and more - are available at www.mises.org *

About the Author

Capping a 20 year career in sales to the Fortune 100, Michael J. McKay founded Iowa Capital Management (ICM) in 1994.

ICM is an investment firm with an international clientèle, where he currently serves as Chief Economist and President.

Michael has been a life long student of how the world works and, specifically, what incentives and motivations cause people to choose to cooperate in harmony with each other - or not.

This naturally led him to study *the integration of* Economics, History, Law and, in particular, Ethics which Michael considers the *foundation* of Law and Economics.

It is Michael's thesis that together these form our Human *Ecology*.

As Ludwig von Mises said,

"...all problems are linked to one another. In dealing with any part of the body of knowledge one deals actually with the whole.

Economics ... invariably deals with all the phenomena of action."

For the past decade Michael has deeply studied and vocally advocated '**Reality Economics**', a term he coined for what academics call '**Austrian Economics**'.

Michael believes we have entered an era where **reality is not optional**.

Understanding this development is required of everyone wishing to survive, and ultimately prosper, in this climate of economic transformation.

Michael is the founder and host of RadioFreeMarket.com